assassination and declared war. Although a small country, Serbia had a powerful friend in Russia. So when Serbia was attacked, the Russians entered the conflict. The **allies** of Austria-Hungary and Russia were drawn in, spreading the war across Europe and beyond.

One small mistake...

When the USA became involved in 1917, the squabble between Austria-Hungary and Serbia had grown into a terrible world war. Was anyone to blame or was it just a series of dreadful accidents? The assassin shot Franz Ferdinand when his car took a wrong turning. Had one small mistake by the archduke's driver changed the history of the world?

ASSASSINATIONS IN HISTORY

'Assassination' means a political murder. The word comes from a group of 12th-century fanatics ('assassins') who killed their enemies as a religious duty. Throughout history, scores of political leaders have been assassinated. Here are some other well-known assassinations:

43 BCE Julius Caesar was stabbed to death by a group of fellow Romans.

1763 Charlotte Corday stabbed to death the French revolutionary leader Marat while he was in the bath.

1865 J Wilkes Booth, an actor, shot dead the great American president Abraham Lincoln.

1963 Lee Harvey Oswald shot dead US president John F Kennedy in Dallas, Texas.

1984 The Indian prime minister Indira Gandhi was publicly murdered by her own bodyguard.

1995 A Jewish extremist shot dead Israeli prime minister Yitzhak Rabin at a peace rally.

The shattered French town of Verdun, which lay on the front line between the French and German armies during World War I. Might all this devastation have resulted from two small pistol shots in Sarajevo?

To die for your country

The nation state

There are over 200 **nation states** in today's world. These are countries that govern themselves. Their people mostly speak the same language and share a common culture and history. In 1914, the idea of a nation state was quite new to most people. Only in the 1860s, for example, had the separate states and cities of Italy been united into a single nation state. A similar process took place in Germany at about the same time. Serbia was a new country, too. Before 1878 it had been a province of the Ottoman Empire.

Nationalism

The peoples of the new states and the older ones, such as Britain and France, were passionately proud

Countries and empires of Europe: 1914

Contents

ssassination!

Two fatal shots

Sarajevo, Bosnia, Sunday 28 June 1914. Beside Schiller's café, on the corner of Franz Joseph Street, a young man gazed miserably across the road. What should he do? His colleagues had bungled the **assassination** and the archduke had escaped. Now the police hunt was on...

About to die: Archduke Franz Ferdinand and his wife Sophie during their visit to Sarajevo. They were shot dead shortly after this picture was taken.

Suddenly, a large open car rounded the corner, stopped and began to reverse. It was the archduke and his party! The young assassin could not believe his luck. Without hesitating, he brought out his gun, stepped forward and fired two shots. The first hit the archduke in the neck. The second ricocheted into his wife's stomach. Both wounds were fatal. This assassination was the trigger for a war that soon engulfed much of the world.

What happened next?

Archduke Franz Ferdinand was heir to the throne of Austria-Hungary, a mighty European power. The government of Austria-Hungary blamed Serbia for the of their countries. This pride is known as nationalism. Nationalists paid great respect to their country's symbols, such as its monarch, national anthem and flag. Children were taught at school to love their country. Newspapers, popular songs and poems all helped increase nationalist feelings.

Wars of independence

Nationalism helped to bind a country together. But it also had its dangers. It could lead people to believe that war was a glorious thing. Extreme nationalists said that it was noble to fight – even to die – for one's country.

Nationalism also inspired peoples who did not have their own country to fight for independence. The Serbs, for example, had been part of the Ottoman Empire since 1459. In 1876, they began a bloody war for independence. They were successful and in 1878 the Ottomans recognized Serbia as an independent nation state.

The Serbian nation prepares to defend itself: Serbian women undergoing military training, 1908.

The sick man of Europe

The age of empire

In the early 20th century, much of the world was divided into **empires.** These consisted of several lands and peoples under the rule of one government. The British Empire, by far the largest, stretched right around the globe. France, The Netherlands, Portugal and Germany also had overseas empires. In and around Europe lay three ancient empires: the Russian Empire, the Austro-Hungarian (or Habsburg) Empire and the Turkish (or Ottoman) Empire.

Nationalism in education: Empire Day celebrations in 1913 at a British primary school.

Empires were set up for several reasons. They could bring wealth and glory to the 'mother country' that owned them. They were also useful markets for the mother country's goods and places where surplus population could go to live. Many British people, for example, emigrated to Canada, South Africa, Australia and New Zealand. Imperial powers (countries with empires) also took over lands to stop them falling into the hands of other empires. This was partly why Europeans divided up Africa in the 19th century.

Imperial families

Some 19th century empires, like the British and the French, were governed by elected **ministers** and their servants. Other empires, like the Russian and the Austro-Hungarian, were governed more personally. The Austro-Hungarian Empire, for instance, was also known as the Habsburg Empire because it was ruled by Austria's **hereditary** ruling family, the Habsburgs.

Imperialism versus nationalism

The imperial powers were eager to increase the size of their empires. This spirit of empire-building is known as imperialism. Clearly, imperialism clashed head-on with nationalism, which inspired peoples to break away from imperial rule. In some regions the clash between imperialism and nationalism had serious consequences.

The sick man

In the 17th century, the Ottoman Turks had controlled a huge empire in eastern Europe and the Middle East. Over time, however, this empire had become weak and started to crumble. Its inefficient rulers failed to adopt new ideas in technology and government. By the late 19th century, the Ottoman Empire was known as the 'sick man of Europe'. Few people believed it would recover.

The vultures gather

Some peoples of the Ottoman Empire, like the Greeks and Serbs, had broken away to become independent **nation states**. Other lands had been taken over by neighbouring empires. Like jealous vultures, the imperial powers hovered over the sick man to see what else they could seize.

Ottoman ruler Abdul Hamid II is unable to stop his empire being torn apart: this French cartoon of 1908 shows Bulgaria declaring itself fully independent while Austria-Hungary seizes Bosnia and Hercegovina.

The powder keg

The Balkans

The Balkans were home to a broad mix of peoples. In this mountainous region ('Balkans' comes from the Turkish word for 'mountains') lived Greeks, Macedonians, Albanians, Serbs, Croats, Bosnians, Bulgarians and Romanians. In some areas, such as Bosnia, several peoples lived alongside each other. There were also two major religions in the Balkans: Islam and Christianity. These cultural and religious differences made the region very unstable.

The break-up of the Ottoman Empire turned many Turkish people living in the Balkans into refugees. A 1912 French magazine illustration.

Imperial rivalry

The Balkans lie at the crossroads between Europe and the Middle East. Here the frontiers of the Ottoman, Austro-Hungarian and Russian **Empires** met. The British also had a strong interest in the area. They did not want it to fall into the hands of a rival power. If this happened, the route through the Suez Canal to India, the jewel in the crown of the British Empire, would be threatened. In 1878, Russia and Turkey went to war. To keep Russia out of the Balkans, Britain threatened to join the war on Turkey's side and so peace was made at the **Congress** of Berlin.

Agreement for peace

Despite the Berlin agreement, by 1900, the Turks had been largely driven out of the Balkans. No imperial power had taken over from them and the region was divided into small **nation states**. There was much rivalry between them, causing the area to be known as the 'powder keg of Europe'. In 1903, worried that the gunpowder might explode, Russia and Austria-Hungary agreed to co-operate to keep the peace there.

FANATICAL HATRED

'We are struck by the feelings of dislike and bitterness which Christians and Mahommedans [Muslims] *feel for each other. There is no other district* [Bosnia] *where the loathing between the Cross and the Crescent is so strong.'*
A report to the Austro-Hungarian government on the conditions in Bosnia, 1875.

Unhealed wounds. Conflicts in the Balkans have yet to be resolved. This 1999 picture shows the devastation caused by the recent troubles in Kosovo, a province of Serbia populated mostly by Albanians. Although the Serbs seized Kosovo from the Turks in 1913, the Kosovar Albanians were never happy to be part of Serbia.

Serbia's advance

Bosnia and Hercegovina

The 1878 **Congress** of Berlin agreed that the Austrians could look after the twin provinces of Bosnia and Hercegovina. This arrangement annoyed Serbia as a large number of Serbs lived there. Indeed, the Serbian government sometimes felt that Bosnia and Hercegovina would be better off as part of Serbia.

Aehrenthal's move

For a long time, the government of Austria-Hungary had been worried by the growth of nationalism in the Balkans. It feared that nationalism would spread into their **empire** and break it up. So, in 1908, the new Austro-Hungarian foreign **minister**, Count Aehrenthal, decided to make a show of strength. He announced that Austria-Hungary was taking over Bosnia and Hercegovina completely and making them part of its empire.

The elderly Austrian Emperor Franz Joseph I (1830-1916). His government's **annexation** of Bosnia and Hercegovina in 1908 raised Serbian fears that they would be swallowed up next.

RUSSIA'S MISSION

Many Russians believed they had a 'mission' to look after their fellow Christians in the Balkans: *'Russia's historical mission was the freeing of the Christian peoples of the Balkans from the Turkish yoke. This was almost done by the beginning of the 20th century. Nevertheless, the young Balkan countries still needed Russia's help if anyone threatened them.'*
Serge Sazonov, Russia's foreign minister, 1928.

Nicholas II (1868-1918), the last **tsar** of Russia. Weak and incompetent, he allowed Russia to be drawn into a war for which it was wholly unprepared.

Fury and fear

The Russians had always been close to the Serbs. They were both Slavic peoples who shared the same Orthodox form of Christianity. The Russians were furious, therefore, when they heard of Aehrenthal's action, but they backed away from direct confrontation. The Serbs were angry, too. They were also frightened. Perhaps they would be next for takeover?

Russia's revenge

To show they still had influence in the region, the Russians encouraged the Serbs to go to war (1912-13). First the Serbs and their **allies** crushed the Turks. Then they turned on Bulgaria. Their victories left Serbia bigger and stronger than ever. They also left Austria-Hungary believing that Serbia was a problem they would have to deal with sooner rather than later.

Beyond the Balkans

Alliances for strength and peace

By 1914, the great European powers were divided into two groups. In 1879 Germany and Austria-Hungary had signed a Dual Alliance. This said they would help each other if they were attacked. Italy joined this alliance, making it a Triple Alliance, in 1882.

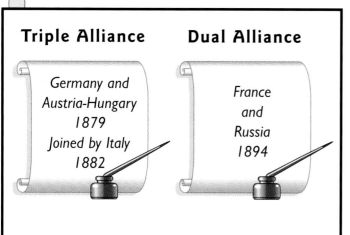

Triple Alliance

Germany and Austria-Hungary 1879 Joined by Italy 1882

Dual Alliance

France and Russia 1894

British Alliance and Ententes

Great Britain and Japan 1902

Great Britain France 1904

Great Britain Russia 1907

The Triple Alliance left France feeling isolated. So, in 1894, it formed its own Dual Alliance with Russia. For several years Britain remained outside this system of alliances. But it too began to feel isolated and in 1902 signed an alliance with Japan. This was followed, in 1904, with an *Entente Cordiale* ('friendly understanding') with France. Three years later, it signed a similar entente with Russia.

In the pre-war years important alliances and ententes were made. Their purpose was to keep the balance of power within Europe.

One world

These alliances and ententes were supposed to prevent war by balancing one side (the Triple Alliance) against the other (the Triple Entente). But they also meant that events in the Balkans impacted in Europe and beyond. What concerned Russia, for example, also concerned her **ally**, France. Furthermore, because of Europe's **empires**, European events affected people worldwide. France's actions, for instance, affected its colonies from Indo-China to North Africa.

Crisis and arms

The alliance system was tested by three serious European **crises** in the early 20th century. In 1905 and 1911, Germany challenged France's right to control Morocco. On both occasions Britain and Russia stood by France and the Germans backed down. As we have seen (page 13), in 1908 Russia backed down when Austria-Hungary took over Bosnia and Hercegovina.

After the 1911 crisis it looked as if the alliance system was working. But all the time the European war machine was growing: larger armies, new weapons, bigger fleets. What was all this for if not war? Would Germany or Russia be prepared to back down again?

'EXPENSIVE LUXURY'

Throughout the 19th century, Britain's Royal Navy ruled the seas. Then, in the 1890s, Germany began building up a powerful navy of her own. British politicians said this was unnecessary (Winston Churchill called it 'an expensive luxury') and feared it would be used to attack the British Empire. In response, Britain increased the power of the Royal Navy. When Germany did the same, an expensive 'naval race' began.

Britain's revolutionary new battleship HMS *Dreadnought*, launched in 1906. Its high speed and huge guns set in revolving turrets rendered all other battleships obsolete. This forced the Germans to build dreadnoughts of their own, so fuelling the costly Anglo-German naval race.

The visit to Bosnia

The Emperor and his nephew

The Austro-Hungarian **Empire** was ruled by the ancient Habsburg family. On the throne in 1914 was the narrow-minded and unsmiling Emperor Franz Joseph I. He knew all about the dangers of being a public figure – his wife had been **assassinated** in 1898. Archduke Franz Ferdinand, the heir to the throne, was Franz Joseph's nephew. He was a cold, hard man, but utterly devoted to his Czech wife Sophie.

The archduke's plans

Franz Ferdinand understood that many of the emperor's subjects wanted to leave the Austro-Hungarian Empire and set up their own independent states. He knew, too, that the Serbs living in Bosnia were among the leaders of this movement. To keep them quiet, he had plans to give them a greater say in their own government.

Archduke Franz Ferdinand, his wife Sophie and their three children. Sophie, a Czech, was deeply unpopular in Austria.

THE BATTLE OF KOSOVO

Briefly, during the 14th century, the Serbs ruled a Christian empire that covered most of the Balkans. But on 28 June (St Vitus's Day) 1389, the invading Muslim Turks defeated them at the Battle of Kosovo Polje. Although a disaster, the heroic feats of that day have inspired Serb nationalists ever since.

Terrorist territory

In the summer of 1914, Franz Ferdinand went to Bosnia to watch the Austrian army training there. At the end of June, he planned a state visit to the important town of Sarajevo. He wanted to impress the citizens and show that he cared about them.

The visit was brave but unwise. Sarajevo was only 80 kilometres (50 miles) from the border with Serbia, and nationalist **terrorists** were known to operate there. The date of his visit, 28 June, was not well chosen, either. It was the anniversary of the Battle of Kosovo Polje, one of the most significant events in Serbian history.

The Bosnian city of Sarajevo in 1893. The assassination took place just off the broad street visible to the right of the river in the top centre of the picture.

Two fatal shots

The Black Hand

Before Franz Ferdinand's visit, Serbian **terrorists** had **assassinated** several Austro-Hungarian officials. When Danilo Ilic, the Sarajevo agent of the Black Hand terrorist gang, heard of the archduke's visit, he signed up six young men and instructed them in assassination techniques. One of his recruits was Gavrilo Princip.

Bomb attack

On Sunday 28 June, Franz Ferdinand and his **entourage** arrived at Sarajevo by train. At around 10 am they left for the town hall in a procession of four cars. As they passed along the Appel Quay beside the river, one of Ilic's young assassins hurled a bomb at the archduke's car.

Gavrilo Princip fired the two shots that killed the royal couple. He is shown here (far right) with two other members of the Black Hand Secret Society.

The archduke's bravery

Showing great bravery, the archduke managed to throw the bomb away before it exploded. Unfortunately, it went off beneath the car behind, injuring several people. The procession now accelerated away towards the town hall. When he arrived, Franz Ferdinand declared angrily, *'So you welcome your guests here with bombs.'* Then he asked to be taken to visit the injured.

Assassination

The route to the hospital was not properly explained to the archduke's driver. He took a wrong turning into Franz Joseph Street. Having heard the news of the failed bomb attack, Gavrilo Princip had left his post and was now standing, quite by chance, outside Schiller's café. He recognized the archduke's car at once. The moment it stopped, he advanced and fired the two fatal shots at close range. Franz Ferdinand and his wife died in hospital fifteen minutes later.

The murder that rocked the world: a contemporary but rather inaccurate artist's impression of the Sarajevo assassination. Sophie was hit by a stray bullet intended for one of her husband's generals.

GAVRILO PRINCIP

Gavrilo Princip, the nineteen-year-old son of a postman, was a member of the 'Young Bosnia' nationalist movement and was fanatically anti-Austrian. After the assassination he took poison. It did not work and he was arrested. Too young to be hanged, he was kept in an Austrian jail until he died of tuberculosis four years later.

The ultimatum

Deadly evidence

Although Princip and the other **terrorists** were Bosnians, their weapons were Serbian. Moreover, several important Serbian officials had known of the **assassination** plot and done nothing to stop it. Armed with this evidence, the government of Austria-Hungary decided to end the Serbian threat once and for all.

German backing

The Austro-Hungarians did not attack Serbia straight away because they were afraid Russia might come to Serbia's aid. So they turned to their major **ally**, Germany, for backing. Many in the German government believed that a European war was inevitable. They were also worried that Russia was getting stronger year by year. Therefore, deciding they had a better chance of victory if they struck first, they gave Austria-Hungary their full support.

A flattering impression of Kaiser Wilhelm II. Advised by his staff, he believed Germany's best hope of victory against France and Russia was to strike first – and fast.

The blank cheque

On 5 July 1914, the Austrian **ambassador** in Germany, explained how the Kaiser promised to back Austria-Hungary against Serbia. The Kaiser's eagerness was seen as a 'blank cheque' of support. *'The Kaiser said…we might in this case…rely upon Germany's full support… It was the Kaiser's opinion that this action* [against Serbia] *must not be delayed.'*

Accept, or else...

The Austro-Hungarian government still did not go to war. Instead, they sent the Serbs a ten-point **ultimatum**. This said they would invade if the Serbs did not give Austria-Hungary complete control over their country. The Serbs had two days to reply.

War

The Serbian government accepted eight of the ultimatum's points. But they refused to accept Austrian officers in the Serbian army or Austrian **ministers** in the Serbian government. This was not good enough for Austria-Hungary and on 29 July it declared war on Serbia.

The Russians prepare for war: infantry exercising with fixed bayonets. The enormous Russian army was seen as a 'steamroller' – slow to start but unstoppable once it had got moving. The image did not take account of the deadly effect of machine guns.

Over by Christmas?

From Sarajevo to world war

When Serbia was attacked, Russia began to **mobilize** its forces against Austria-Hungary. In response, on 1 August Germany mobilized its forces and declared war on Russia. France, Russia's **ally**, began preparing for war. Keen to strike first, Germany then went to war with France. When German troops moved into **neutral** Belgium, on 4 August Britain declared war on Germany.

Death but not glory: British troops going 'over the top' during the Battle of the Somme, 1916. Ordered to walk calmly towards the enemy lines, 60,000 men were killed or wounded in the first day's attack.

Inspired by feelings of nationalism, millions on either side rushed to join the army. They believed the war would be 'over by Christmas' and they did not want to miss it. They were tragically mistaken. Neither side managed to get the upper hand and other nations were drawn into the conflict. By Christmas 1915, Turkey, Italy and Bulgaria had entered the war. The USA, threatened by German aggression, finally joined in April 1917. The European war was now the first ever world war.

The two sides in World War I	
ALLIED POWERS	**CENTRAL POWERS**
France	Germany
Britain	Austria-Hungary
Russia	Ottoman Empire
Italy	Bulgaria
USA	
Serbia	
Montenegro	
Romania	
Greece	
Portugal	
Japan	
Brazil	

War of attrition

The war dragged on until November 1918. This was partly because, before the entry of the USA, the two sides were equally matched. Another reason was that defensive weapons were superior to weapons of attack. Machine guns, barbed wire and trenches made it almost impossible for foot soldiers to attack successfully. The result was a ghastly war of **attrition** as each side tried to wear the other down.

Total war

The war produced horror on a scale never seen before. The casualties were enormous. The hardships endured by soldiers living and fighting in cramped and unhygienic trenches were unspeakable. Moreover, the conflict affected everyone, soldier and civilian. Millions were **conscripted** into the armed forces and other war work. Bombing attacks from aircraft and airships put **civilians** at home in direct danger. Food was **rationed** and all available industry was geared towards winning the '**total war**'.

Breakthrough

At the end of 1917 Russia withdrew from the war that had caused a bloody **revolution**. Germany's forces could now concentrate on fighting Britain, France and the USA. But by then, years of war had taken their toll on all the warring nations.

In the end, Germany was defeated because it was overwhelmed. A naval blockade prevented Germany importing food and raw materials. American forces, backed by new offensive weapons – the tank and aircraft – finally gave the Allies (principally Britain, France and the USA) sufficient power to break the stalemate and force the Germans to surrender.

The horror of war: Italian soldiers carry a wounded comrade to safety after the Battle of Gorizia, 1916. Despite joining Germany and Austria-Hungary in the Triple Alliance in 1882, Italy entered the war on the side of the Allies in 1915.

The lost generation

Casualties

It is estimated that the war killed 1.8 million German soldiers and wounded a further 4.2 million. The figures for Russia were 1.7 million killed and almost 5 million wounded. For France they were 1.38 million killed and 4.2 million wounded, and for the British Empire 0.95 million and 2.1 million.

Many of those killed in the fighting were young volunteers, the flower of their country's manhood. When they did not return home, their families spoke of them as the 'lost generation.'

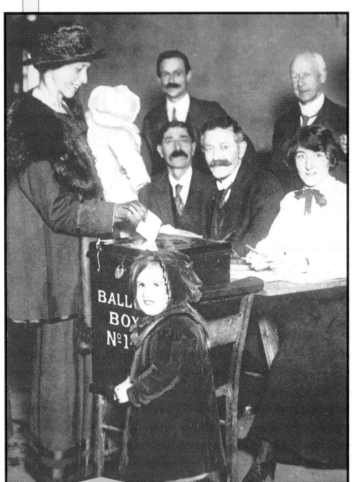

British women voting in a general election for the first time, 1918. The right to vote was seen as a kind of 'reward' for the vital work millions of women had done during the war.

Pacifism

The war was followed by an outbreak of influenza that killed as many people as the fighting. Europe was shattered and demoralized. In the late 1920s, a stream of anti-war novels and poems appeared. The most famous was Erich Remarque's novel *All Quiet on the Western Front* (1929). Some who grew up in this post-war world were **pacifists** who believed all war was wrong.

Women prove a point

Only a few women had taken part in the fighting. But millions suffered when their countries had been invaded or through the loss of husbands, fathers, brothers and sweethearts.

In one way, however, the war helped women. With most young men absent on the battlefield, they had successfully taken over men's jobs. This helped change attitudes towards women's rights. Between 1914 and 1939, in twenty-eight countries worldwide women won the right to vote.

THE WAR POETS

Soldiers who openly criticized what was going on during the war risked being shot as cowards or traitors. However, some expressed their private feelings of disgust in poetry. One of these was the British officer, Siegfried Sassoon.

Suicide in the Trenches

I knew a simple soldier boy
Who grinned at life in empty joy,
Slept soundly through the lonesome dark,
And whistled early with the lark.

In winter trenches, cowed and glum,
With crumps and lice and lack of rum,
He put a bullet through his brain.
No one spoke of him again.

You smug-faced crowds with kindling eye
Who cheer when soldier lads march by,
Sneak home and pray you'll never know
The hell where youth and laughter go.

Siegfried Sassoon, 1918

Wilfred Owen, war poet and friend of Siegfried Sassoon. Unlike Sassoon who survived the war, Owen was killed just one week before the Armistice was signed. His vivid, realistic poems, published after his death, were influential in changing people's attitude to war.

A war to end all wars?

The empires collapse

Many governments collapsed under the strain of **total war**. When the fighting went against them, the European **empires** of Russia, Austria-Hungary, Turkey and Germany crumbled. Britain and France were exhausted and almost **bankrupt**. In contrast, the war left the USA indisputably the wealthiest and most powerful nation on earth. As a result, the post-war world looked very different from that which had gone to war so confidently in 1914.

Revolution in Russia

The **revolution** early in 1917 replaced Russia's ruler, the **tsar**, with a Western-style government. Unwisely, it continued the war, leading to a second revolution in the autumn. This brought to power the world's first **Communist** government. The Communists murdered the tsar and remained in power in Russia for over 70 years.

Tsar Nicholas II gives up his throne in 1917, having lost the respect of almost every section of Russian society. His path to disgrace is lined by the ghosts of countless dead Russian soldiers. The cartoon is doubly ominous: the next year Nicholas and all his family were murdered by the revolutionary Communist government.

New states

The victorious **Allies** held a series of conferences to sort out post-war Europe. They divided the Austro-Hungarian and Ottoman Empires into **nation states**. Austria and Hungary, for example, became separate countries. The small Balkan states, including Serbia and Bosnia, were formed into the new country of Yugoslavia.

The victors decided Germany's fate at the Versailles Conference (1919). They blamed it for causing the war, reduced it in size, took away its overseas colonies and ordered it to pay £600,000,000 to the victors in compensation.

The new world

The Allies announced that the war had been 'the war to end all wars'. They hoped to avoid future conflicts by punishing their defeated enemies and setting up the **League of Nations** to keep world peace. Neither policy worked. The League had no power to stop aggressors. Many Germans felt deeply humiliated. Some dreamed of revenge. In 1933, they chose a leader who promised them that revenge: Adolf Hitler.

GERMANY'S FAULT?

The **Treaty** drawn up by the Versailles Peace Conference blamed Germany for starting the war. The Germans were forced to accept this blame.

'Germany and her allies accept responsibility for causing all the Allies' wartime loss and damage, which came about as a result of the war brought upon them by the aggression of Germany and her allies.'

[From the Treaty of Versailles, simplified.]

The ultimate consequence of World War I? Hitler's Nazi brownshirts at a rally in 1933. Hitler's popularity stemmed partly from his promise to restore German pride after the humiliation of defeat and the effects of the harsh Treaty of Versailles.

Causes and blame

What if?

Historians are interested in events, their causes and their consequences. Asking 'what if?' is not really their job. But it can sometimes help us understand why something happened. For example, what if Princip had missed? Or what if the Archduke's driver had not taken a wrong turning? Might World War I never have happened?

The countries of Europe after World War I.

Just one spark...

Some people believe tiny events, like the driver's mistake, can have enormous consequences. Others believe small incidents have little influence. They point out, for instance, that for years Europe had been quietly talking about war and preparing for it. It needed only a spark to set it off. That spark happened to be the **assassination**. But it could just as easily have been something else.

Whose fault?

Historians, like the politicians, have tried to find someone to blame for World War I. Recently, they have pointed the finger at the Kaiser's government for offering unlimited support to Austria-Hungary. This was certainly unwise. But so were many other things, such as the **ultimatum**, Russia's **mobilization** and the arms race in which all countries took part.

Though the causes of the war were very complicated, what we do know for certain is that the events in Sarajevo on Sunday 28 June 1914 acted as a trigger, starting a chain of events which rapidly led the world to war.

WARNING IGNORED

In *The Great Illusion*, first published in 1909, Norman Angell warned the countries of Europe that war would solve none of their problems. Tragically for Europe, his words were ignored.

'…it is impossible for one nation to seize by force the wealth or trade of another – to enrich itself by subjugating, or imposing its will by force on another;…in short, war, even when victorious, can no longer achieve those aims for which peoples strive.'

[Synopsis of the 1911 edition.]

Lest we forget: row upon row of soldiers' graves, each representing a wasted life and broken dreams.

Time-line

1871	German Empire set up	
1879	Germany and Austria-Hungary join in a Dual Alliance	
1882	Italy forms a Triple Alliance with Germany and Austria-Hungary	
1894	France and Russia join in a Dual Alliance	
1904	Britain and France settle their differences in the Entente Cordiale	
1905-6	Crisis in Morocco. Germany backs down.	
1907	Britain and Russia sign an entente	
1908	Austria-Hungary takes over Bosnia and Hercegovina. Russia objects but backs down.	
1911	Second crisis in Morocco. Germany again backs down.	
1912-13	Serbia gains from two Balkan Wars	
1914	28 June	Assassination of Archduke Franz Ferdinand
	5 July	Germany's 'blank cheque' to Austria-Hungary
	23 July	Austria-Hungary's ultimatum to Serbia
	29 July	Austria-Hungary attacks Serbia
	30 July	Russia prepares for war
	1 Aug	Germany declares war on Russia
	3 Aug	Germany declares war on France
	4 Aug	British Empire declares war on Germany
	Nov	Turkey joins Germany and Austria-Hungary (the Central Powers)
1915	May	Italy joins Britain, France and Russia (the Allies)
	Oct	Bulgaria joins the Central Powers
1916	March	Germany declares war on Portugal
	Sept	Bulgaria attacks Romania
1917	April	USA declares war on Germany
	June	Greece and Brazil join the Allies
1917	Communists come to power in Russia	
1918	Nov	Armistice ends fighting on the Western Front
1919	Treaty of Versailles between Germany and the Allies. League of Nations set up. Treaty of St Germain ends the rule of the Habsburgs. US Senate rejects the Treaty of Versailles; US backs away from European affairs.	
1920	Treaty of Trianon breaks up the Austro-Hungarian Empire. Treaty of Sevres breaks up the Ottoman Empire.	
1933	Hitler comes to power in Germany	

Glossary

ally, allies	an official friend and helper in time of trouble
ambassador	someone who represents their country in another country
annexation	to take possession of a country or piece of territory
assassinate, assassination	to murder, usually in public for political reasons
attrition	wearing something down steadily bit by bit
bankrupt	a state of financial ruin
civilian	anyone who is not a member of the armed forces
Communist	someone who believes that the state, not individual people, should own all important industry, property and wealth
congress	an international meeting
conscription	when people are forced to join the armed forces
crisis	a time of danger (the plural of crisis is crises)
empire	many lands governed by one country
entente cordiale	a friendly agreement or understanding
entourage	a group of people looking after an important person
hereditary	inherited by members of the same family
League of Nations	an organization established in 1919 to try to prevent war. Now replaced by the United Nations.
minister	a member of a government
mobilize	prepare armed forces for war
nation state	a country united by a single language and culture
neutral	not taking sides
pacifist	someone who believes that all use of force, particularly war, is wrong
ration	to limit food supplies in time of war or crisis and share them out equally between people
revolution	a quick, complete and permanent change
terrorist	a person who uses violence and intimidation to try and get their way
total war	war that involves a country's industry, agriculture and civilian population as well as its fighting forces
treaty	a written agreement between countries
tsar	an emperor of Russia before 1917
ultimatum	a final demand that must be obeyed to avoid punishment or retaliation

Index